Table Settings

SPECIAL TOUCHES FOR ENTERTAINING

Mary Forsell

AND THE EDITORS OF

Victoria

MAGAZINE

Hearst Books

New York

Library of Congress Cataloging-in-Publication Data

Forsell, Mary
    Table settings / by Mary Forsell and the editors of Victoria magazine.
        p. cm.
    ISBN 1-58816-052-1
        1. Table setting and decoration. I. Victoria (New York N.Y.) II. Title.
TX871.T75 2002
642'.6–dc21   2001039860

Printed in Singapore

First Edition 2002

10 9 8 7 6 5 4 3 2 1

For VICTORIA MAGAZINE
Editor in Chief: Margaret Kennedy
Creative Director: Cynthia Hall Searight
www.victoriamag.com

Design by Alexis Siroc
Produced by SMALLWOOD & STEWART, INC., New York City

Contents

Foreword

Nothing gives me more pleasure than setting a table for family and friends — unless it's enjoying their company around that table. Having a variety of tableware to play with, according to mood and season, is such a passion that my cupboards fairly bulge! Whenever I discover a new pressed-glass goblet or some irresistible antique pink lustre dessert plates, the possibilities only expand. Not that everything matches. For a large buffet, I'll use different sets of plates and silverware. For small sit-down parties, a collection of white china gives me many color choices. Often it's based on what's blooming in the garden: If pale pink peonies are ready to star, it's a day for the pink linen tablecloth.

This book is about just such possibilities. You may be moved to throw a luncheon under a leafy arbor or place a present at each table setting: I sometimes cluster little pots of primulas in a basket as a centerpiece, then let my guests take them home. And if you're something of a traditionalist, as I am, you'll enjoy reading about the history of table manners and fashions as well.

Often, as I put the final touches on the table, I remember how my mother wouldn't think twice about inviting anyone who was around to dinner. She set a pretty table, too, but what made it truly beautiful was her easy spirit of sharing. At *Victoria,* we think that's what entertaining is all about.

Peggy Kennedy

EDITOR IN CHIEF, *VICTORIA*

Starting the Day

You don't need to be expecting company to set a special breakfast. On a table for two, serve juice in a crystal carafe, let French toast preside in a footed compote, and tuck cutlery in a vintage cream pail. We applaud the hostess who heeds Mrs. Beeton's timeless advice: "Always have a vase of freshly gathered flowers on the breakfast table and, when convenient, a nicely arranged dish of fruit."

An overlooked opportunity to entertain, breakfast is a marvelous way to celebrate a birthday, an anniversary, or the Saturday-morning arrival of a weekend guest. Unlike lunch or dinner, its service is not dictated by conventions — at least not in this century. You are free to set the table in any number of ways depending on your whim. Choose the porcelain soup plates from your dinner service for cereal bowls, for instance, and serve the juice in claret glasses. Or employ a collection of cow creamers not for its intended purpose but as "bud vases" at each place setting.

Just by pulling up a single element of unconventional seating, perhaps a stool, a picnic bench, or even a church pew, you can completely change the look of a table. In this case, a Louis XVI bergère imparts a more substantial air to a casual breakfast. Though formal in style, the armchair's elegance is softened by its bold checks, which keep it compatible with the ladder-back rush seating. Simple country touches come from an enamelware pitcher and wire-work egg basket — classics that are still being produced today.

More often than not, breakfast guests don't appear on your doorstep — they straggle downstairs, lured by the robust scent of coffee. A buffet glistening in morning sunlight will be a most welcome sight. All you need do is set up a sideboard with tableware the night before and get the coffee brewing first thing in the morning. The meal can be as basic as croissants and muffins in a silver cake basket, a tray of fresh fruit slices arranged in fan shapes, and pretty pewter mustard pots of marmalade and jam. It will seem like a five-star luxury to your guests, but it takes just minutes to do.

Even if you or your houseguests are late risers, don't let breakfast become lunch in disguise. Take advantage of all the irresistible breakfast-related paraphernalia that became popular in the nineteenth century, when the Victorian penchant for formality and

garden plants, tucked in small, moss-filled terra-cotta pots, can greet guests with a personalized tag at each place.

natural objects such as shells or river stones can be monogrammed with a paint pen.

one special dish will show you care: for instance, line a bowl with mint leaves and top it with a pyramid of strawberries.

local maps and guides, perhaps annotated with your own comments, would be a welcome morning touch alongside each guest's coffee cup. Include disposable cameras so everyone can record the day.

specialized servers resulted in such novelties as silver grape holders, orange cups, and banana stands.

In your antiquing travels, keep your eye on the whimsical: perhaps a fluted silver-plated egg coddler topped by a hen or a sectioned breakfast tray with covered compartments, each lid with a fanciful handle. Look for Staffordshire transferware in tried-and-true informal color combinations such as red and white, blue and white, and brown and white. The beauty of this kind of tableware is that it all goes together effortlessly and dresses up a simple breakfast of eggs and toast. Even the most homespun pancake breakfast will take on a special quality when you serve it with a pierced silver pancake server, a nineteenth-century object that can still be found in antiques shops.

Choose also from a wide range of delightful twentieth-century breakfast ware: streamlined Art Deco services complete with teapot, toast rack, milk jug, and hot water pot; chrome jam cruets from the 1920s; and an endless parade of cheery juice glasses that enlivened breakfast tables at midcentury.

though this serve-yourself spread (above) looks elaborate, it is really nothing more than a few simple elements artfully arranged. Equipped with a pretty lace cloth, a fruit basket, and a tiered stand, even the most time-pressed hostess can quickly gather together a welcoming buffet. Think of the fun in finding an egg personalized with your name nestled in a silver cup. The eggs (opposite) are lettered with a gilt felt-tip marker. Supply the local newspaper, and your guests will settle into vacation mode.

room service

In the English country house tradition, houseguests awaken to covered trays discreetly left outside their bedroom doors. But you needn't be a guest to enjoy a small, luxurious breakfast.

Set a tray with silver and a wrapped gift (top left) for Mother's Day or a birthday. Lavish the tray with other special touches, like a dish of candied ginger or herbed butter.

Treat yourself to your favorite books and homemade cookies (bottom left), in a basket to be carried outdoors.

A tray for your beloved is too small for a grand bouquet, but charming sprigs of sweet flowers such as lily of the valley (opposite) can fill an orphan teacup.

The First Cup

As coffee is prepared with art, so one should drink it with art," advises an Arab adage. The drinking of coffee can be a ritual as refined and pleasurable as that of drinking tea.

First, consider your coffee accoutrements. Drip coffee makers are convenient, to be sure, but an old-fashioned percolator or even a streamlined French press makes a more graceful presentation. Though glass and ceramic are preferred over metal for serving coffee, there are aesthetic exceptions—a 1930s hotel silver coffee service, for example, or an Art Nouveau pot.

While coffee pots themselves are usually recognizable by their straight sides—in a matching service, they are always larger than teapots—many whimsical designs have been created. Look for pear-shaped Staffordshire pots, antique ceramic pots with animal paws for feet, or pots decorated with a family's coat of arms or monogram with matching cups (above left).

Convention dictates that the strength of the brew determines the size of the cup. Morning and lunchtime coffee, which tend to have a smooth, light body, are traditionally sipped from larger cups and mugs (opposite) and generously sized pottery (above right). Strong-tasting, thick-brewed coffees such as espresso are taken from smaller cups: demitasse cups if it's a formal occasion; after-dinner coffee cups, which are slightly larger, if the affair is more casual.

Alfresco Entertaining

FOR MANY OF US, INFORMAL ENTERTAINING IS THE STANDARD PROTOCOL. AND WHEN MOTHER NATURE COOPERATES, NO ONE CAN RESIST THE CHARM OF A RELAXED MEAL ON THE TERRACE OR UNDER AN OLD SHADE TREE. BEFORE FRIENDS ARRIVE, YOU NEED TO DO LITTLE MORE THAN LAY THE TABLE WITH A CLOTH AND SOME FLOWERS. THE KEY IS TO EMPLOY TABLEWARE AND FURNISHINGS YOU ALREADY HAVE ON HAND IN CREATIVE — MAYBE EVEN FRIVOLOUS — NEW WAYS.

Dinner on the lawn?

Cocktails on the terrace? Brunch in the treehouse? Entertaining doesn't always have to take place in a dining room. When you give your imagination freedom to seek out other possibilities, entertaining becomes a creative process—part of the fun of celebrating—rather than a logistical puzzle.

Perhaps there's a corner of your yard that would lend itself to an afternoon gathering. If the roses are blooming and the butterflies visiting, turn the potting shed into a serving area for a garden party. Add sturdy poles with hooks to raise a makeshift tent overhead (it could be something as simple as an Indian-print cotton bedspread); set tiki torches around the property; string paper lanterns from the trees, glowing with tiny white lights. Another possibility is to mark the boundaries of your party "room" with lanterns made by standing candles in mason jars filled with sand.

Create with items you already have on hand. For instance, set up "stations" at an outdoor buffet by arranging a grouping of small tables. A washtub could become a generous ice bucket for Champagne. For centerpieces, try something unconventional. Pots of sea grass marching down a picnic table would be charming at a clambake, perhaps with a hurricane lamp in the center surrounded by seashells. Fill a spongeware bowl with sea urchins. Carve several pumpkins as candleholders for a harvest celebration; for added color,

Fallen branches make rugged stakes for an outdoor dining canopy. Punch grommets into the corners of the fabric and thread twine through each to wrap the branches. Fanciful cottage teaware, an early-twentieth-century collectible, keeps the mood playful. A fringed shawl makes an ideal casual table covering.

The Italian passion for long, leisurely meals and spirited conversation dates back at least to the sixteenth century. With their temperate climate, Italians have been perfecting outdoor dining for just as long. The earthenware and rustic serving pieces they use every day are ever so appropriate, segueing gracefully from lunch to dinner, from indoors to out (opposite). ❧ Tableware taboos only get in the way of creativity. Paper napkins are considered too casual by some, but in fact many are of high quality, printed with fresh motifs, and are quite acceptable for alfresco dining. Just a dozen or so flirty lily of the valley napkins perk up a simple serving tray (right). What an appealing way to present cocktails or lemonade!

cluster savoy cabbages in rich mossy greens and electric purples. Fill a clear glass pantry jar with clementines. A parade of heirloom tomatoes might be lined up along the center of a canvas-topped picnic table.

When the weather doesn't permit an outdoor affair, you can bring that same casual spirit indoors. Even the most formal dining room can be dressed down. Under a boldly striped tablecloth, your triple-pedestal mahogany dining table becomes far less imposing. Coarsely woven linen or hemp fabric has a rustic, Provençal aura; pair it with hand-thrown plates and bowls. Dress a table with gingham-checked fabric, top it with ironstone pitchers and English rolling pins. For an instant table runner, cut yardage right off the bolt and layer it on in varying widths. Try ticking in marine shades as a foil for your Blue Willow china.

breezy bouquets

Anyone can arrange flowers that have an easygoing charm. Try sunflowers in a watering can, butterfly weed in a vintage coffeepot, gerberas in a painted bucket.

Why limit yourself to one vase when you can enjoy half a dozen? Vintage milk bottles in their original metal carrier (top left) still look charmingly rustic beneath a drift of garden roses.

Nestled in a straw sun hat, bundles of freshly snipped herbs (bottom left) make an offbeat, fragrant centerpiece for an outdoor luncheon.

Mix wildflowers with cultivated blooms to balance nature. The jolly graphics of an olive oil container (opposite) offset the formality of any flower.

Dressing Down

Table linens needn't be starched, pressed, and intimidating. For instance, when you choose a loose-weave linen with stripes in an unexpected color like pink (opposite), you bring a relaxed air to the table. Rather than an all-white scheme, pair a printed cloth with white damask napkins for a casual look (above left).

So many textiles lend themselves to creative adaptation—vintage French dish towels with classic red banding (above right) are a case in point. Let the shape dictate the function. Square ones make nice place mats. Longer, narrow types are perfect as table runners. If you find a supply of vintage kitchen linens in similar colors, treat them as napkins, combined perhaps with a classic striped Basque country tablecloth. Use them also to line cocktail trays and baskets ready to be filled with muffins and breads.

Blankets make unexpected table dressing. For a cozy winter dinner or an autumn cookout by the lake, toss them over tabletops; dress the chair backs with colorful fringed throws. Ticking, too, is a classic rough-and-tumble material that makes a facile transition to the table. Originally the covering for mattresses, linen and cotton ticking is durable and designed to take some wear, which is why it's such a perfect choice for a summer-house. It partners nicely with gingham napkins and cheerful pottery at lunch or white linen napkins and china for a candlelight dinner.

or a summer dinner party that begins with cocktails in the barn, one imaginative hostess asks each of her guests to grab a chair and carry it to the field, where a long harvest table awaits. The drama comes from the surprising contrasts: a slipcovered armchair set in a meadow, white china, the palest amethyst wine glasses, etched goblets, and a humble linen mesh cloth. To cover odd-size tables such as this one, cut fabric off the bolt to the desired length, let the selvage edges hang off the table's sides, and fringe both of the cut ends.

Pressed Glass

Most cupboards in American homes hold a few pieces of old pressed glass. Mass-produced in the nineteenth century as an elegant yet affordable alternative to handblown glass, pressed glasswares were made in such vast quantities that even a humble household could boast a sparkling fruit bowl or compote.

America's earliest pressed glass is known as "Lacy," so called for its ornate scrolled, spiral, and botanical designs reminiscent of lace. Because the basic glass-pressing process produced many bubbles and flaws, the intricate decoration was added to camouflage the imperfections. Boston and Sandwich, one of the best-known makers of the style, was most prolific from 1820 through 1840.

The period from 1865 to the Edwardian era is considered the golden age of pressed glass, when a new formula made glass easier to press quickly and inexpensively. An explosion of patterns emerged, complete with fanciful names: "Snail," "Ribbon Candy," "Argonaut Shell," "Pearls and Scales," and dozens more.

Color also arrived on the scene; novelty wares like Victorian shoe whimsies were decorated with a dark amber or ruby stain. Custard and carnival

glass, inexpensive stand-ins for art glass, were also in demand. By the early twentieth century, Victorian frippery was passé, and pressed-glass designs became simpler. Trends reversed in the 1930s, and Victorian pattern glass, as the intricate designs of the era are known, were widely copied. A catchall term for this era is Depression glass, which is any pastel glassware made from 1925 to as late as the 1960s. The period also added its own repertoire of patterns, including hobnail, etched designs, and Art Deco-influenced geometrics.

Some collectors doggedly hunt down a single pattern; others collect by theme. Pressed glass is especially versatile, lightening the mood of a table, mingling as easily with blown crystal and fine china as it does with its own kind.

Indulging in Tea

CELEBRATION, CEREMONY, MEDITATION: ACROSS CULTURES

AND ACROSS TIME, THE SIMPLE ACT OF TAKING TEA HAS BEEN

CALLED MANY THINGS AND INTERPRETED IN COUNTLESS WAYS.

DEPENDING ON YOUR INCLINATION, IT CAN BE A CHATTY

GET-TOGETHER WITH FRIENDS, A FIRESIDE RENDEZVOUS

À DEUX, OR A TRANQUIL RESPITE AT A TABLE SET FOR ONE.

YOU NEEDN'T BE A VETERAN TEA DRINKER TO CREATE THE

MOOD AND TAKE PLEASURE IN THE AESTHETIC.

Instead of having a spot of tea, think in terms of a spot *for* tea. Where you choose will completely determine the mood and the accessories. Tea alone by the fire could be simply enjoyed, steaming from a mug wrapped with a rustic napkin. For tea with friends on the front porch, set the table with heirloom floral china, along with a few pieces of celluloid- and ivorine-handled cutlery.

Tea for twenty on the lawn is another affair entirely: You might go formal, with linen napkins edged in ecru lace, gleaming silver and cutlery, delicate tongs to serve crustless sandwiches, and, for the crowning glory, a neoclassical silver tea urn with lavish engravings designed to catch the light. Or you could just let whimsy reign, with a chorus of unmatched cups and saucers.

If you want to entertain a large number of guests with ease, consider the dessert party, a perfect opportunity to show off a collection of elegant pedestal cake stands. Stack the stands —all in silver or crystal or milk glass—in pyramids in order of decreasing size; arrange one with sugared fruits and nuts, another with petits fours, a third with chocolates in fluted-paper cups. For variety, alternate square cake stands with round ones.

At a dessert party, you may want to serve iced tea instead of hot tea. Feature decorative glassware, such as candy-stripe Murano, clear-stemmed pieces, or gold-trimmed etched French tea

Think of each teatime as an opportunity to orchestrate a table service of seemingly incompatible pieces. With a dessert tea, a rare pressed tin cake pedestal can become the perfect mate for a more graceful white china pattern. What brings harmony to the pairing is the scallop edging the stand and pottery share.

Unlike delicate china tea cups, stoneware mugs evolve from the tradition of high tea — in England the workingman's light supper of lunch leftovers. In spring, serve high tea with pastel stoneware mugs and napkins (right). ❧ Teatime is a happy excuse to set out coordinating accoutrements, using a single theme as your guide. A four o'clock table (opposite) recalls an afternoon at the seashore when laid with shell-motif silver and blue-and-white transferware.

glasses. For each glass, provide a clear or colored Italian glass swizzle stick. Display those iced tea sippers — silver straws with little spoons at the end — that you found at the flea market. Of course, this is also a chance to show off your glass pitcher collection, accessorized with sprigs of mint and bobbing slices of oranges and lemons.

Though tea cuppings — taste evaluations similar to professional wine tastings — are rare today, they're another wonderful way to share this beverage with friends. Offer a few classic examples of the three kinds of tea: green, oolong, and black. Let guests sample brews from individual pots, savoring the subtleties, grading the different varieties according to cupping's time-honored language ("toasty" refers to aroma; "winy" to the mellowness; "brisk" to the "live" quality of the tea). Take this opportunity to showcase a collection of interesting pots, from cottageware to Chinese celadon to a 1930s James Sadler & Sons English teapot shaped like a roadster. Tea is so much more than a drink!

In an American garden, a teahouse was conceived with architectural elements that echo those of old European summer cottages (left). Though unheated, the three-season hideaway is oriented to the sun so that it seems toasty even on sunny December days. Simple furniture designed to withstand the elements — wicker, teak, rattan — and a few topiaries and pillows create a spot for daydreaming. An afternoon tea, also known as low tea, requires only the daintiest serving pieces to present its de rigueur crustless sandwiches and cakes (above).

Sweet Presentations

Perhaps it was tramp art and the popularity of primitive collectibles that drew our attention to wirework. On a well-set tea table, these simple, utilitarian wares are now as chic and prized as porcelain. When wire wares were mass produced, they became a part of every bourgeois household in Europe as well as America. Egg baskets, trays, pedestal stands (above left), fruit and pie domes, cooling racks (above right), trivets—the pieces came in a seemingly endless array of shapes and purposes.

Today, the intricate wire patterns make a perfect decorative stage for presentations of foods, especially sweets. A fruit basket decorated with brass beads becomes a holder for scones and muffins. Geometrically shaped tiered racks, originally designed for allowing just-baked pies to cool, hold fresh fruit or tarts or simply present plates filled with tempting teatime creations. Even something as mundane as a hanging dish drainer with a central niche for cutlery is transformed into a basket for fancy cookies surrounding a flower arrangement. A rectangular oyster basket with a wooden handle serves biscotti. And egg baskets are ideal for presenting macaroons, madeleines, and meringues.

Many new wire baskets are just as handsome as the originals. Some are actually spectacular: One artist created a cake dome festooned with antique glass beads (opposite).

Nature's Splendor

NATURE IS INFINITELY SPLENDID, AND FLORA AND FAUNA
ARE THE MOTIFS OF SOME OF THE MOST ELEGANT CHINA.
DECORATING WITH A NATURAL THEME IS AS AMBITIOUS AS
A GRAND TABLE SERVICE DEVOTED ENTIRELY TO A SINGLE
FAVORITE FLOWER—PERHAPS VIOLETS, PERHAPS ROSES. IT IS
ALSO AS SIMPLE AS A TUMBLER OF THE THINNEST GLASS,
EXQUISITELY ETCHED WITH A CLASSIC GRAPE MOTIF. PEARS,
STRAWBERRIES, BUTTERFLIES—ALL OF NATURE IS ART.

Buds, blooms, branches of berries, and other

natural elements are a china designer's best friend. Twining across time as slowly and surely as an old wisteria vine on a Southern veranda, these motifs have long been tabletop favorites. Witness the continued popularity of a classic pattern such as "Napoleon Ivy." Originally made by Wedgwood in 1815, this tableware features nothing more than a simple border of ivy leaves. Even today, it serves admirably on the table during any season, paired perhaps with a centerpiece of ferns in summer, evergreen branches in winter. So, too, "Feuille de Choux," or cabbage ware, continues to delight as it did in Sèvres, France, in the eighteenth century. Named for its raised borders resembling the ruffly edges of a cabbage leaf, the gilt floral china will always be at home at spring garden parties.

Of course, some patterns are no longer made, and finding them becomes a treasure hunt. Rather than the perfect match, consider a complementary pattern, for just as in nature, botanicals will coordinate if they share a provenance, or a motif, or a color palette. Fearlessly combine cottage rose china with chintzware; don't hesitate to marry winged themes like birds and bees.

Collectors can't get enough of the vividly glazed pottery known as majolica. Cauliflower-shaped tureens, lettuce-leaf plates, "wicker" baskets filled with fruit molded in relief, decorated

In lieu of more conventional framed Redouté images, plates inspired by antique botanical drawings decorate a dining room. On the shelves of a vivid blue cupboard, a collection of dinner plates, soup plates, dessert plates and chargers, teacups, sugar bowls, cream pitchers, finger bowls—even a variety of etched crystal glasses—is totally mismatched yet completely harmonious. What brings this all together? Nature, of course.

Impressive indeed is a full table of "Queen Victoria" (opposite). The pattern is also exceptionally rare and costly. Happily, just a single piece—such as a tureen—will energize an all-white setting. 🐚 At first glance, the cherry motif at the center of Coalport porcelain dessert plates predominates (above). But a closer look reveals tiny molded flowers on the rim, a classic fillip of English makers. 🐚 Fruit and chestnut bowls made in the nineteenth century frequently had pierced or perforated patterns with painted flowers in relief at the intersections (above right).

seashells resting on painted nests of seaweed—the range of trompe l'oeil designs is remarkable and convincing. The majolica popularity blossomed in 1851, and makers from all over Europe and America quickly contributed patterns, not just in botanical motifs but in animal shapes like monkeys, parrots, cats, and fish.

While naturalistic dinnerware brings the outdoors in, there are many other elements to cultivate the atmosphere. For spring, consider a pastel garden palette: lilac dishes, a lavender silk tablecloth, and gentle green glassware. Set off with real flowers and a potting bench as a sideboard, the scheme brings the season into your dining room. When you combine contrasting textures — a cherrywood charger, an Indonesian teak tray, spun bamboo baskets, flatware with mother-of-pearl or bark-style celluloid handles, beeswax candles — you create an aura of tranquil rusticity.

pattern potpourri

One secret to mixing an array of china swirling with petals and leaves? Choose a common color. Gold is a classic choice; it acts as the unifying "peacekeeping" force for a varied stack (opposite).

Green has been called nature's neutral for its ability to go with anything and soften the edges of disparate designs. Grass-hued glass dessert bowls and beakers (top left) bridge the pattern play between teacups and plates.

To highlight the nosegay painted in the center of a lovely dish, frame it with a plain dish set beneath it. Austere white dinnerware layered between two ornate patterns (left) eases the transition from one motif to the next.

Plates from Nature

For Provençal potter Mireille de Reilhain, seeking the muse is never an elusive task. Her inspiration resides in all of nature, whatever the season. "I take walks through the countryside as often as possible, in the early morning or the end of the day, and I always find something new to stimulate my work," says Mireille, who works in a stone outbuilding located in a former vineyard.

She is perhaps best known for her mastery of the ancient Provençal technique of terre mêlée, or "mixed earth" (above left). "You have to mix clay with powdered pigment, then let it dry to a point that you can work with it," Mireille explains. "Next the potter marbleizes the clay by blending layers together. In the past, potters used just one or two colors, but I've reinvented the tradition by using five, six, or as many as I like. In winter, I'm drawn to cool blue shades. Autumn always prompts a deeper, terra-cotta–type palette."

In sunny Provence, people dine outdoors much of the year, and Mireille designs her tableware with this in mind. "I am often asked what sorts of centerpieces complement my work," says Mireille. "I tell them to fill a glass bowl with water and white lily heads floating upright, surrounded by bay leaves and citrus fruit. Or set wheat sheaf bouquets on the table with creamy white tapers in silver candlesticks. A much simpler possibility is to surround a gourd with olive branches [opposite]. Nature, I find, can be dressed up or down."

the seasons

Bittersweet vines twine down the center of a harvest table (left). The silk taffeta runner, a particularly appropriate cloth for autumn, resembles crewelwork.

Spring's grape hyacinths and sweet peas are diminutive enough to be displayed in a goblet (opposite top left).

Dinnerware patterned with starfish, scallop shells, and nautilus shells reflects high summer (opposite top right).

Berry-bright colors, lacework snowflakes, and fanciful figurines add warmth to the winter table (opposite bottom left).

In fall, candelabras join lush garden bouquets. Paisley fabric and oriental-patterned bowls capture the tapestry of changing foliage (opposite bottom right).

Flora Danica

In the land of the midnight sun, flowers grow abundantly during the warmer months of the year, nurtured by light all day long. In winter, gloom lasts for months at a time; how Scandinavians long for the sight of their heathered fields and cherry orchards. It makes perfect sense, then, that Flora Danica, or Plants of Denmark—one of the world's most famous sets of porcelain—was created. Conceived as a gift for Catherine the Great of Russia by Crown Prince Frederick of Denmark in 1790 and completed in 1802, the set contained almost two thousand botanically accurate plates rimmed in 18-karat gold.

Today, Flora Danica is in production through Royal Copenhagen, and reproductions of all the course-specific tableware from the past are still available, from relish plates (opposite, at center) to reticulated openwork bowls (above left) to saucers, triangular salad bowls, and, of course, teaware (above right). Each piece has the botanical name of the plant it depicts inscribed on the bottom.

If you display a highly decorated botanical service like Flora Danica, go easy on your other tabletop adornments. For centerpieces, all you may need are simple ivy or myrtle topiaries, or perhaps moss set on stones in a low bowl. You might replace a centerpiece with ivy tendrils entwined in a wrought-iron chandelier. Or simply light a row of beeswax candles, just as the Danes would do to celebrate the art of dining.

White as Clouds

ECRU, EGGSHELL, SNOW, BISQUE, PORCELAIN: THERE ARE

COUNTLESS SHADES OF WHITE. PURE, PEARLY TONES

ARE COTTAGEY AND LIGHT, FRESHENING UP WHATEVER

THEY SURROUND. IVORY AND PARCHMENT LEND A MELLOW

SENSE OF AGE. WHITE IS A CHAMELEON, FROM REGAL

TRIMMED WITH GOLD, TO FLIRTATIOUS PAIRED WITH PINK.

WITH WHITE AS THE FOUNDATION OF YOUR TABLETOP AND

DINING AREA, YOU'LL ALWAYS HAVE THE PERFECT SETTING.

All white china loves its own company, whatever its motif, shade, and shape. So when a hostess looks for a pale palette in her collecting travels, she is building a storehouse of endless mix-and-match possibilities. The undisputed queen of the table, of course, is porcelain, the true china, so translucent that when you hold it up to a light, you can actually see your fingers on the other side. What began as a rare ceramic from the Orient was, after many false starts, successfully manufactured in Europe, and now we have the opportunity to collect the vast legacy of makers from the eighteenth century onward. One need not limit porcelain to the most elaborate and formal dinner parties, however. A breakfast tray for two, laid with graceful porcelain teacups and saucers, shouldn't be considered an indulgence. A luncheon table set with a wonderfully mismatched array of white porcelain plates, perhaps bearing gold monograms and family crests, has a fresh, unmatchable personality that elevates even modest foods to the level of indulgence.

By the same token, don't allow yourself to be biased by any tableware's humble origins. Milk glass, for instance, was created in the nineteenth century as an affordable substitute for porcelain, creamware, and other sought-after tableware. From hobnail goblets you can press into service as vases to cake stands with latticework borders (many designed to be displayed with ribbon woven through

More perhaps than people in other cultures, Scandinavians appreciate the allure of white, which lightens rooms as it brightens the spirit on the darkest winter day. In a Swedish dining room, white is merely a catchall term for the many nuances at play (opposite). Simply painted wooden chairs are the hue of pure snowdrifts, while the sideboard captures the deeper tones of seafoam in a turbulent tide. With its gold rims, the china echoes both the color of the mirrored sconce and the buttery shade of the candles.

Just as white makes a small room look larger, it brings a sense of openness to an intimate table. Several shades of white are at play in such a palette (opposite), from ivory on the chair and woodwork to the clotted cream of the china and linens. ❧ Designers of china have always delighted in adding decorative motifs, such as elaborate pierced borders and ribbon-inspired patterns (above), to the rims of plates. ❧ White softens the impact of even the boldest shapes (right). Contemporary pottery would seem strident in a bright color, but in a pale glaze, it is a study in serenity.

the perforations) to oil lamp bases that flank a sideboard, milk glass of many vintages is still widely available, lending its creamy gleam to almost any occasion or interior.

White porcelain and creamware have another virtue: Any and all of it can shine throughout the house. Hang plates on walls, arrange fresh bouquets in pitchers, heap seasonal ornaments in tureens for centerpieces. Smaller white vases are supremely versatile — on a desk, filled with freshly sharpened pencils, or on the vanity, holding brushes for makeup. Perhaps a few identical vases keep forks, knives, and spoons stylishly separated, in an economy of space. A serving tray slipped behind the faucets of the kitchen sink makes a beautiful backsplash. In the living room, another tray works as a magazine holder, at once containing and displaying periodicals. If white is your passion, your options are endless.

Creamware

Just about anyone can recognize "Wedgwood blue" jasperware, decorated with romantic Greek mythical scenes, but it was cream-colored earthenware, introduced in the early 1760s, that made Josiah Wedgwood one of England's wealthiest men. The fourth-generation potter lightened the natural mustard color of Staffordshire earthenware by hand-washing the unpurified clays to produce an appealing warm white; the addition of flint also increased the whiteness. To this he added a clear glaze that concealed surface blemishes. Originally called Wedgwood, the pottery was so beloved by Queen Charlotte that it was renamed, in her honor, Queen's Ware.

Of course, most people just called it cream-ware, because its warm buff color reminded them of clotted cream. Within a matter of years, Wedgwood's invention became so popular that European makers responded with their own versions of creamware, called *faience fine* or *faience anglaise*. On Wedgwood's home front, keen competition came from the Leeds Pottery of Yorkshire, England. The Leeds glaze is glassier than Wedgwood's, and in certain lights can have a greenish tinge (look for the color especially in crevices, where glazes puddle). Leeds's major innovation was piercework, not just on the rims of tea and dessert plates, but also to ornament baskets and candlesticks, centerpieces and urns. Cut by hand, hole by hole, the patterns of diamonds, hearts, lozenges, and petals have been compared to lace in their intricacy.

Today, collectors tend to mix it all, leaning toward tablescapes of milk jugs, punch pots, relish pots, reticulated plates, and teapots with sprigged work, no matter what its origin. If you're searching for antique Wedgwood creamware, keep in mind that its heyday lasted until 1820, when the company introduced a whiter-toned china called pearlware—which happens to mix beautifully with creamware. Ironically, early creamware, once so affordable for all, is expensive today. (Beware imitations marked "Wedgewood.")

Creamware continues to be produced by a variety of makers, with the same piercing and white-on-white work that goes so well in any setting (opposite). Mix it with salt-glazed stone-ware or porcelain on a tabletop with only pale china, or use it with pastels—lavender, peach, seafoam—for an ethereal, watercolor look.

Clever is the hostess who combines pretty with practical. For the airiest and most efficient buffet, tuck ivorine- or celluloid-handled dessert forks and pale organza napkins in Champagne flutes so that guests can easily serve themselves (above). Hand-blown glasses etched with a laurel swag "frame" their contents. Entertaining with white doesn't preclude color. On a table set for a tête-à-tête for good friends (right), the tablecloth and cushions contribute touches of pale silvery gray.

The Delights of Linens

Once a prerequisite for every bride, artfully stitched linens with lace trim and eyelet borders were designed to endure.

And so they have; vintage linens can be found today at various venues. Among the most captivating are monogrammed designs (above). When you discover a cache of monogrammed textiles in your antiquing adventures, by all means scoop them up, regardless of the letter they depict or even the purpose they serve. All can be brought to the table with charming results.

For instance, an 1920s batiste sheet lavishly embroidered can serve as a tablecloth or even as an outdoor canopy. Monogrammed tea towels from the 1930s can "slipcover" café chairs—

simply fold them over the tops of the chairs and anchor them with ribbon tied through the hem-stitched openings. Initialed linen handkerchiefs stand in for napkins at tea. Sturdy linen dish towels with cross-stitch embroidery, in imitation of aristocratic crests, were popular in the nineteenth century; today they make homey place mats.

If you plan to store linens for a long period, avoid starch, which can attract insects and cause the fabric to deteriorate. Store them in a cool, dark armoire or hope chest. Folding antique linens weakens the fabric; store them flat or rolled. Never use plastic bags, and line your drawers; unbleached muslin is ideal. Tuck in a lavender or dried rose petal sachet.

History's Allure

There's something so poignant about vintage tableware. Perhaps it's that people sat at table with these heirlooms, to chat about the day's events, celebrate the family's milestones, appreciate the companionship of friends. And because a piece has survived decades and even centuries, you know it has been cherished by each successive generation. Today, the tradition of treasured history carries on.

A tabletop heirloom can mystify even the most astute social historian, its original purpose obscured by time. But it wasn't that long ago when silver lamb chop holders, pickle dishes, and compotes provided exotic table garniture.

The art of dining reached its pinnacle in the nineteenth century. It was at this time that the word *gastronome* came into parlance. It was the age of Jean-Anthelme Brillat-Savarin, the self-styled authority on *l'art culinaire.* Cooking schools thrived throughout England, and Mrs. Beeton's books were best-sellers.

In those banquet years, the number of courses served easily numbered eight or nine. At a grand estate, butters, aspics, and jellies were molded into elaborate forms. A typical manor house menu might include a sequence of hot and cold consommés followed by filet of trout, quail with grapes, glazed chicken studded with truffles, then a saddle of Welsh lamb garnished with peas à l'anglaise. Next would come a salad and a table delicacy like ortolans (finches, that is). For dessert, you could have a sweet soufflé, quivering jellies sculpted in towering fluted molds, petits fours, coconut sponge cake crowned with cherries, and — just to add to the culinary cacophony — canapés of anchovies! Each course, naturally, was accompanied by a change of wines: clarets, Burgundies, Champagnes, and after-dinner port, sherry, and vintage Cognac.

For affluent Victorians, both the food and tableware were designed to spark engaging dinner conversation. In an English manor house dining room, a French porcelain dessert service handpainted with views of the Continent would have inspired lively recollections of trips abroad. The jellied desserts sat on the table during the entire meal, for guests to admire.

pierced cake baskets are so delightful, they should be put out as often as possible. Let them hold flowers and fruit, as well as vegetables of the season, such as baby peas and carrots in spring, pumpkins and tiny squashes in fall.

biscuit barrels and muffin baskets can serve as ice buckets at your next party.

antique toast racks aren't just for breakfast. Try them as napkin holders or to sort the family's mail.

ice cream trays with matching saucers and "ice canoes" — boat-shaped glass bowls — are elegant ways to serve olives or hors d'oeuvres.

Of course, all this sounds terribly excessive, but the dishes themselves tended to be petite, slightly larger than modern-day tasting portions, and guests were not necessarily expected to dine on each course. In fact, the point was the presentation. Displayed on table and sideboards, these artistic creations prompted a custom called "the tour of the tables," led by the host and hostess prior to dining, as Napoleon III and Eugénie were wont to do.

Inevitably, with all these courses and ostentatious foods, the trappings of the table grew enormous. Today we needn't restrict eccentric pieces to their original purposes. For instance, crystal celery vases make dramatic holders for pillar candles. Pierced silver mustard pots become lovely containers for jams and sauces and even tiny flower arrangements. Delicate wineglasses from the past can hold sorbet or melon balls. A fine pot de crème set can be turned into a centerpiece, each individual cup filled with fresh flowers, holiday candy, or favors. If an object is beautiful in its own right, you'll most certainly discover a new role for it.

though the size of the place setting has evolved over time, utensils are always arranged from the outside in. In a French setting (opposite), the forks and the soup spoon are placed upside down to show off the decorations on their backs, and dessert utensils sit horizontally above the plate. ❧ Ready for luncheon, the table in a formal dining room (above) takes on an air of festive playfulness with splashes of ruby- and cobalt-colored crystal atop an otherwise all-white setting.

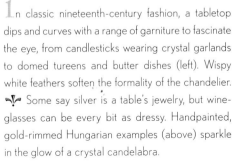

In classic nineteenth-century fashion, a tabletop dips and curves with a range of garniture to fascinate the eye, from candlesticks wearing crystal garlands to domed tureens and butter dishes (left). Wispy white feathers soften the formality of the chandelier. ❧ Some say silver is a table's jewelry, but wineglasses can be every bit as dressy. Handpainted, gold-rimmed Hungarian examples (above) sparkle in the glow of a crystal candelabra.

Table Gems

We can credit the Victorians for the exquisite colored glass that collectors so prize today. In 1845, the Glass Act, which had made English glass prohibitively expensive, was repealed. As a result, demand for colored and engraved designs soared. And, as was so often the case, the appetite for these new collectibles traveled across the Atlantic. Both English and American companies turned out shimmering creations that surpassed even the legendary workshops of Bohemia thanks to new, more sophisticated methods.

Much of it was designed to mimic the brilliance of valuable gems and metals, and was named accordingly. Ruby glass is a term often interchangeable with rubinglass. Amberina glass gradates from yellow to ruby. Burmese gently shades from pink to pale yellow. Uranium glass is named for the ingredient that gives it a distinctively yellowish-green color. Mercury glass was made as an inexpensive alternative to real silver.

To achieve these marvelous colors, a variety of techniques was developed. One of the most popular, flashing, involved dipping clear glass into molten liquid to create two layers of glass. An artist would then carve motifs on the top layer to reveal the clear layer beneath. Enameling, gilding, applied glass threading, and many other elaborations were also common.

What resulted was a remarkable array of designs for every conceivable purpose. Previously made only in silver and clear glass, epergnes were created in cranberry-colored glass and suddenly became all the rage. Ruby-flashed biscuit barrels, faceted aperitif glasses, amethyst beaded-dart goblets, and blue sorbet coupettes all glowed in jewel-box shades.

opulence *Bohemian cut glass dates from a seventeenth-century tradition. Though its popularity faded over time, it enjoyed a revival in the nineteenth century with the introduction of even more spectacular colors. Ruby red-flashed glass with cut motifs (top left) was considered a pinnacle of the art.*

sparkle *An emerald decanter (bottom left) is faceted like a gem. Set amid clear glass, it becomes a mesmerizing focal point, bringing the enchantment of a glittering chandelier to eye level.*

color *Fearlessly mix different shades and palettes. Or create an all-ruby setting (opposite), accented with red-checked linens and red transferware.*

gold and white

New Wedgwood that
revives patterns from the past
is more affordable than
vintage, and it has the same
charm (top left). Combine
it with gold place mats.

In noble European families,
even everyday dinnerware
is white and gold (bottom left).
On your antiquing jaunts,
pick up any gold-rimmed pieces;
they needn't match.

Collecting teacups can become
an unmanageable obsession,
but if you narrow your focus
to a single color scheme or motif,
a compatible set is virtually
guaranteed (opposite).

Handmade Silver

Handwrought silver is a rarity, but there is a handful of artisanal makers who faithfully continue the tradition. In Paris, the workshop of Souche Lapparra is a European legend. Within its walls, top-quality silver is still made by the hand-hammering method to produce historic patterns, some dating back as much as two hundred years. With origins in the eighteenth century, a silver Louis XVI vegetable dish is one example, its floral flourish as detailed as nature's own. The shop's thousands of historical, ornate patterns—complete with tiny scales, serpentine twists, and miniature though expressive gargoyle faces—simply cannot be rendered in such lilliputian detail in a machine-made world.

Old Newbury Crafters in Amesbury, Massachusetts, is another stellar source of silver; in fact it is the only commercial workshop of its kind in the United States. At Old Newbury Crafters, the process of silversmithing has not changed in the fourteen generations that the company has operated. Their studio is a bit of a throwback to the Victorian era, when there was flatware for every conceivable purpose. They still make tomato spoons, grapefruit spoons, fish serving forks, and custom work of all kinds. It takes forty-five minutes to make a teaspoon, and eight hours for a punchbowl ladle. Each piece is personally signed by the craftsman. And it is guaranteed to appreciate in value.

163

138

Collecting Silver

There's a world of silver to collect, both entire matched sets and odd pieces. Bud vases, toast racks, creamers, marmalade spoons, cake knives, asparagus and sugar tongs, and salt cellars are among the jumble of silverware you'll typically find at markets, priced so reasonably as to be irresistible.

Among the most sought-after pieces are British silver and silver-plated items such as napkin rings, teapots, decanter labels, and sauceboats. During the last quarter of the nineteenth century,

these objects were imbued with mythological or romantic motifs such as gods and goddesses, cupids, and other exotic figures. Today, they make charming conversation pieces.

Look, too, for the magnificent wares of eighteenth- and nineteenth-century Boston artisans. Particularly prized are candlesticks sporting details such as hexagonal and octagonal bases and shell motifs on the bobeches. Nineteenth-century Russian silversmiths are acclaimed for the extraordinary level of workmanship they achieved. Available now at antiques shops are *kovshy*, or single-handled drinking vessels, as well as bread baskets and cigar cutters. Names like Sazikov, Ovchinnikov, Morozov, and Nicholls & Plincke are the most well known.

After 1860 all American sterling was labeled as such; it usually carries a manufacturer's hallmark. If the word "sterling" appears, it could also be an Irish piece made after 1720. If the word "England" is present, it was made after 1891. Earlier British pieces usually are marked with a series of tiny pictures, including a lion denoting sterling. Pieces with numbers on the back (800, 900, etc.) are usually Russian or European.

function *Originally designed as a milk ewer, a silver piece (opposite) has a timeless grace that encourages service on any table, from breakfast to a formal dinner.*

ingenuity *Silver napkin rings (top left) were crafted in the most ornate designs. Some included bases to elevate the napkin from the tablecloth.*

personality *Antiques dealers usually have clutches of spoons, forks, or knives, each in an individual pattern (bottom left). Collect patterns that you admire, and feel free to use one of each in every place setting.*

Off the Table

You'll always remember the thrill of the discovery — the moment you found that favorite ironstone platter or the creamer that is a perfect match to your rose-covered teapot. When you entertain with these pieces, memories are rekindled, pleasures revived. For the hostess who invites her collections to reside in all the rooms of the house, special serving pieces become everyday joys.

Perhaps the greatest challenge of table-setting is artfully arranging the dining room and kitchen tables for everyday life. You want them to look interesting, yet be virtually maintenance-free. Fortunately there is absolutely no rule that dictates a tabletop must be outfitted with a crystal fruit bowl flanked by two candlesticks. Instead, set that pair of candlesticks within a glittering constellation of candleholders of different sizes and materials: crystal, glass, metal, pottery. To bring the look together, rely on neutral, identical candles, such as classic ivory-toned beeswax tapers.

Any bare tabletop can become a poetic setting with some imagination. A collection of wooden spools of varying sizes makes for an architectural tablescape. Snake a collection of colored glassware down the center of the table in a serpentine fashion. Let a cake salver display a collection of found natural objects — moss, acorns, pods, and stones. A shallow pewter bowl full of carpet balls with a red and white theme makes a cheery accent on a breakfast table. Even a vintage dollhouse with its tiny furnishings or a series of miniature birdhouses can take up residence on the table.

Before mounting a plate collection on a wall, designers suggest playing with the elements on the floor. Begin at the center with the largest piece — most often it's a platter — and create an "orbit" of dinner plates, saucers, and unusually shaped objects such

Crystal goblets and colored glassware would hardly seem extraordinary massed in a china cabinet, as is their typical off-table presentation. But when you take a few extra minutes to line them up in formation in a niche, they take on a sculptural, even graphic air. Pink hydrangeas bring a splash of much-needed color.

How does one hang a pastiche of plates that go together? Focus on a single color or motif. Blue, in all its nuances from robin's egg to royal, is a versatile common denominator (opposite). They couldn't be more different in styling, but American scroll-edge milk glass, English transferware, French Limoges porcelain, and Italian giltware plates harmonize beautifully. ⑤ Flowers — both real and painted — are the unifying element of another tableau (right). The vase, cup, and pitcher also share a bond: the handles on each create a pleasing rhythm .

as half-moon relish dishes. If you like, work the pieces into a shape, such as a triangle or a circle. You need not strive for absolute balance; professionals rely on a degree of asymmetry to surprise the eye and keep it moving around the design.

When choosing plates for display, the group is more interesting when it is not limited to a particular era or maker. Mix and match them on the wall or in a cabinet just as you would on the table — perhaps a blend of blue-and-white Delft, chinoiserie, and faience. Side-stacking plate racks are a marvelous way to contrast interesting rims — for instance, a collection of transferware — while also keeping them handy.

ather than creating a solitary centerpiece, one hostess whipped up a series of focal points (left). Peonies, lilies of the valley, and sweet peas are arranged in ordinary drinking glasses. In the background, tureens scale a wrought-iron stand and pedestals show off a girandole and assorted pots. ✺ Dramatic glass candlesticks act as everyday tabletop sculpture (above). During dinner, the candlesticks stay in place, unlike a tall floral centerpiece, which would obstruct the view.

blossoms
and glass

*If you dine in the sunroom,
create a tablescape of crystal,
which multiplies the natural light.
An etched decanter makes a
lovely bud vase (left).*

*Take tea amid a sparkling indoor
garden. Glass cloches (opposite)
nurture fragile plants, but
they can also serve as domes to
cover plates of tiny pastries.*

*Float freshly picked blossoms in
shallow glass bowls filled with
rose water. Select bowls according
to the size of the flower heads.*

Shelf Life

With their flat shapes that lend themselves so naturally to wall hanging, plates and platters make decorating easy. But three-dimensional items like bowls, vases, and pitchers present more of a challenge. To group these disparate shapes with harmony, limit the palette and you'll have a foolproof display.

In one example, heirloom ironstone and contemporary polka-dot pottery share space in a cabinet (above right). In such a case, the palette isn't so much a single color as a cream-and-pastel mood. Don't think the arrangement is random! To satisfy the eye's love of balance, plates are stacked on either side of a sauce tureen. Canisters flank a "dishscape" of plates and bowls.

The same holds true for a rose-and-white grouping. Though the results are sophisticated, the approach is simple: As if you're building a miniature city of blocks, stack plates and saucers, cups, and bowls (above left). Allow distinctive pieces, such as creamers and ewers, to stand alone. Plates act as a backdrop, almost like wallpaper.

Another distinctive collection for display, perhaps even more spectacular, is a grouping of vintage children's china (opposite). Not to be confused with doll furniture, these pieces were made as true replicas of conventional dinnerware, though they were scaled for the small hands of children. They served at youngsters' parties, and today bear their chips and scratches proudly.

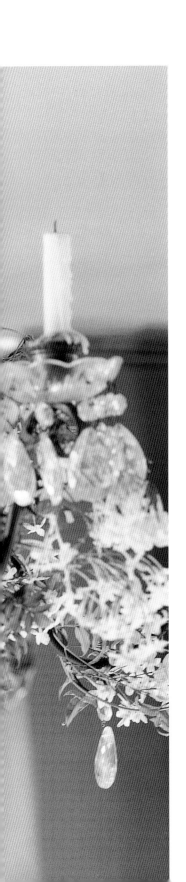

Special Occasions

To celebrate life's milestones and everyday wonders,

create an atmosphere as extraordinary as the menu.

Just as you cook more creatively, decorate more

daringly. Dangle shell, pearl, and crystal necklaces

from a chandelier. Toss white rose petals over a table.

Though weddings, anniversaries, and birthdays come

to mind, a luncheon with an old friend and dinner

for two are also reason enough to make magic.

More than any other decorating element, color sets the mood when you're entertaining. And when you select a particular palette and dare to be bold, you'll achieve striking effects that suit the drama of special occasions. Imagine, for instance, a stunning two-color theme. Matte white art pots are filled with white and purple lilacs. On a majestic white platter, virtually black tulips intermingle with bunches of lustrous Concord grapes. The table service is a symphony of amethyst goblets, pure white china, and mother-of-pearl-handled flatware. Granted, this is hardly the type of arrangement for a casual dinner party, but at a noteworthy anniversary or birthday occasion, the theatricality would be absolutely appropriate. In fact, it's just right.

Experiment with unusual centerpieces and tabletop elements, many of which might be found in your garden or around the house. A lush wreath, for instance, can be positioned on the table, and its center filled with visual intrigue. A grapevine wreath might encircle pillar candles of varying heights. A clear glass bowl can be lined with orange slices, with peach roses or fresh sunflower heads arranged in the center. A similar effect is achieved with a glass vase filled with cranberries, which anchor the fresh flowers. Or forego flowers entirely; instead, stack fruits and vegetables on tiered stands or hollow them for votive candle holders.

An easy though dramatic way to dress a cake: Position it on a pedestal stand. Then create a garland of edible petals from pesticide-free roses, borage, and violets. To enhance the effect, place pale lavender sugar dots over the top and sides of the cake.

seek out pressed glass cake stands from the nineteenth and twentieth centuries. Not only were they made in green, yellow, and blue, they also came in a variety of shapes: Square and cloverleaf designs proliferated. Stack colors and shapes, each container filled with pastries, nuts, and candied fruits.

nestle a checkerboard of truffles and silk flowers in a heart-shaped candy box.

delight children with apothecary jars of confections: white chocolate–covered cherries, bubblegum balls, peppermint sticks, and licorice whips.

construct "strawberry trees" by spearing whole fruits with toothpicks to topiary bases.

Specialize in the offbeat and the unexpected. At a wedding or an outdoor party, invert wine glasses and tuck a place card and a single anemone underneath each one. Enlist terra-cotta pot bases as chargers, decorative tiles as small serving plates, and flat, slate-like rocks as serving boards. On warm evenings outdoors, leave a paper folding fan at each setting.

Let your tablecloths take a more festive and innovative turn. For a sense of luxury, layer them. In winter, for example, toss a plaid lap blanket or a paisley shawl over a solid-colored fabric. Interesting wallpaper remnants could serve as runners. Or swathe the table in a fantasy fabric, such as shimmering aqua floral tulle.

Think off the table. Even the most ordinary slatback garden chairs become exceptional when their backs are strung with garlands of just-picked daisies. Add a touch of eyelet ribbon, and

When a china pattern inspires an entire tabletop, the effect can be dazzling; blue and white was the starting point for a buffet (opposite). The flatware is bundled together with the napkin and secured with a floral fabric tie. 🙿 For an appealing dessert table, exaggerate the presentation. In one case, cake and cheese domes mingle with garden cloches (above). The tallest display is a masterwork of cake stands stacked two high, crowned with a vase of roses enclosed in a bell jar.

a home wedding is the most extravagant celebration of all, and one classic theme is winter white. For this event, the focus is not so much on the dining table or a buffet, but is spread lavishly around the house, so every corner is magical (opposite). Graceful armchairs invite guests to linger and chat comfortably. When it's time for the Champagne toast, everyone can reach for a glass on the mantel, where more lilies "frame" the scene (right). The wreath above reinforces the pale palette with touches of silver and celadon.

you'll have created a dreamy rites-of-spring effect. For the Christmas holidays, hang a stocking of favors from each chair. For New Year's Eve, swag costume jewelry along the backs for glitter and glamour. Even the chandelier is dressed with crystal beads, vine tendrils, a ribbon cascade, colorful paper lanterns, or feather butterflies.

For a romantic party, ornament a banister with a garland of sweet annie, wild grasses, sage, and small bouquets of yarrow and tansy. Bunch the bouquets together with florist's wire. Wrap the wire around the base of each bundle; conceal the join by overlapping the next bouquet. With fresh flowers—hydrangeas, eucalyptus, and roses—the technique is the same, the flowers kept fresh with stems in florist's vials. The scent—and the effect—are pure heaven.

When they spot a chandelier dangling from the tree, flaunting trinkets that include spectacles and crystals, guests know this is no ordinary picnic (left). Hampers and plates wear tie-on linen covers. The table itself has a tiered skirt of vintage crocheted cloth and floral fabric. 🌿 If you have a birthday or anniversary to celebrate, organize a surprise outing for a small group of friends. A casual split-wood picnic basket (above) makes the perfect carrying case in which to hide an exquisite lattice-iced party cake.

please be seated

A manila tag doubles as a place card and gift tag when it's dressed with a fern frond and attached to a beribboned token on a plate (opposite top left).

Calligraphic place cards might also sport small drawings, stenciled motifs, or paper-punched designs (opposite top right).

Tucked within an organdy napkin and embellished with gold ink, a place card takes on the mysterious air of an unopened letter (opposite bottom left).

For a ladies' luncheon, trim place cards with lilies of the valley and prop them on herbal nosegays held in silver tussie-mussies (opposite bottom right).

When you next entertain, create a flickering light show not just on the dining table but throughout your home. Float votives in a pottery punch bowl; introduce the theme outdoors with glowing lanterns. Candles decorated with foliage wink and gleam on a silver tray, which can be transported anywhere for instant aura (above). ❧ Artfully displayed on a tiered stand, honeycomb votives and roses, two natural partners, shake up the usual order with the inspired choice of white turnips (right).

Napkin Rings

A Victorian invention, napkin rings began as strictly utilitarian items, intended to identify napkins individually so they didn't have to be laundered after every meal. Figural napkin rings of silver plate were especially popular. Each family member had his or her own ring, often designed to reflect hobbies and interests.

Lately there has been a revival of interest in napkin rings, not just in collecting older examples, but also in hostesses creating new ones from simple materials, tailored to special occasions. For Thanksgiving dinner, cluster eucalyptus, autumn leaves, cinnamon sticks, and dried sage. Tie the aromatic bundles together and cinch them around a napkin with raffia for a rustic look. Christmas napkin rings could feature leaves of fresh holly tucked under a band of grosgrain ribbon. If you like, add sprigs of festive pink pepperberries. For a New Year's Eve celebration, wire and twist together strands of prestrung glass beads and faux pearls, then wrap the jewels around a linen napkin.

Possibilities build with the seasons. Spring means nosegays of lilies of the valley or violets, held around the napkins with slips of ribbon.

For those casual get-togethers when mismatched dinnerware sets the table, rifle through the sewing basket for any kinds of odds and ends, snippets, and trinkets that you could put together for a home-crafted country look. Jolly rickrack could tie flatware to napkins; beaded or silk flowers attached to covered elastic bands would be sweet at a picnic.

When the occasion calls for pure elegance, consider fabrics that are wildly impractical, just for the sheer luxury of it all. Raw silk, organza banded with satin, taffeta trimmed with velvet—each would be a gesture at once grand and unusual.

linen *is as appropriate for the ring (opposite) as it is for the napkin itself. Originating with Victorian practicality, a tiny slip of linen can be embroidered and simply tied around a napkin.*

natural elements *need not be confined to the botanical. Feathers (top left), shells, and even wish bones can be transformed into napkin rings.*

raffia *is undeniably the most popular material for tying together ornaments, place cards, favors, and flowers for snappy napkin rings (bottom left).*

Romancing the Napkin

"*The silver dish-covers reflected the lighted wax candles in the candelabra, the cut crystal covered with light steam reflected from one to the other pale rays; bouquets were placed in a row the whole length of the table; and in the large-bordered plates each napkin, arranged after the fashion of a bishop's mitre, held between its two gaping folds a small oval-shaped roll.*"

So wrote Gustave Flaubert of a mid-nineteenth-century French banquet featuring the extravagant practice of decorative napkin folding. The Victorian era inspired napkin folds as intricate as origami, often taking on the fanciful shapes of animals, boats, and hats. It's amusing to revive and renew many of these classic folds, finessing them with small touches for a contemporary air. So gather a napkin potpourri—monograms, dish towels, and embroidered and gossamer designs. See how a few simple folds can let you create fantasy on a plate.

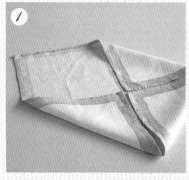

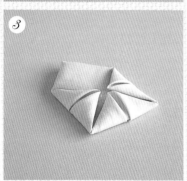

The Blossom All by itself, this fold looks like a flower blooming atop a plate; it also makes a pretty cradle for a flower or gift poised in its center. We chose a 15-inch square white napkin with a contrasting pink border that echoed the pink rose we planned to set at the center. The rose, its stem cut short, floats in a small bowl of water. Once seated, a diner places the bowl alongside her plate as a table decoration, then shakes the napkin out for her lap.

1. Lay the napkin face down, and fold all four corners to the center, forming a smaller square.

2. Fold all four newly formed corners to the center, forming an even smaller square. Lightly press with your palms.

3. Keeping the folds in place, turn the napkin over. Fold all four corners to the center, forming yet a smaller square. Lightly press with your palms.

4. Reach under each corner and pull out the flap from below, allowing the napkin to "bloom."

The Easel Tuck a place card, favor, or greeting into this versatile design. Or go natural with feathers or flowers. To make a generous easel, we started with a 26-inch square linen napkin. Starching and ironing the napkin after making each fold will give you a crisp easel that holds its form.

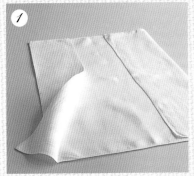 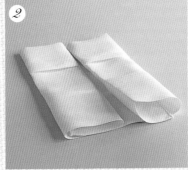 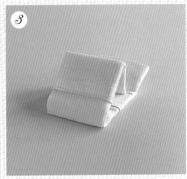

1. Lay the napkin face down. Fold in the left and right edges a little more than halfway toward the center. Spray with starch and press.

2. Turn the napkin over. Fold in the left and right edges halfway to the center, then fold them in again to meet at the center. Spray with starch and press.

3. Fold the napkin in half, as if closing a book, and press. You'll have one long rectangle. Fold each end in to meet the overlap, making two flaps, and press. Fold the napkin in half and press. Stand the easel upright by overlapping the two flaps.

The Soufflé

Cotton or linen napkins work well for this casual fold. Include a little bouquet of flowers or herbs—diners can't resist plucking up the bouquets and enjoying their fragrance. This napkin is 18 inches square.

1. *Lay the napkin face down. Fold it in half by bringing the bottom corners up to meet the top corners. Fold the napkin in half again, to make a square, bringing the left edge to meet the right edge. Fold it in half again, to make a rectangle, bringing the left fold to meet the right edge.*

2. *At the end closer to you, slip both thumbs between the top two layers. Cuff the napkin twice, as if rolling up a shirtsleeve. Gently open the napkin to form a tube, and stand it with the cuffed end as the base.*

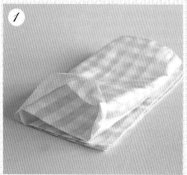 

The Button Tie

Napkin ring and fold become one and the same with an idea based on string-tie envelopes. Sew buttons on a set of napkins, or on a collection of vintage dish towels (their oblong shape is just right for protecting laps when a casual meal isn't eaten at the table).

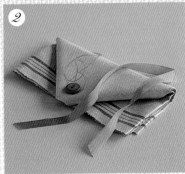

1. Fold the napkin twice, to make a square, and press with a warm iron. With a dish towel, fold it as needed to make a square — or as close to a square as possible. Fold two corners in to make a triangle on one side, and press.

2. Fold the napkin in half, bringing the triangle over as if closing the flap of an envelope. Position a button near the tip of the flap, slip the needle and thread once through the top layer, unfold the napkin, and sew on the button; then refold. Cut a length of bias seam binding long enough to wrap around the napkin, with extra for each end to wrap once or twice around the button.

$\mathscr{P}$hotography $\mathscr{C}$redits